TICKET TO THE

TRIPLE CROWN

T0062252

MARTIN GITLIN

ADMIT ONE

THE BIG GAME

YOUR FRONT ROW SEAT

45TH PARALLEL PRESS

Published in the United States of America by Cherry Lake Publishing Group
Ann Arbor, Michigan
www.cherrylakepublishing.com

Reading Adviser: Beth Walker Gambro, MS Ed., Reading Consultant, Yorkville, IL
Book Designer: Jen Wahi

Photo Credits: Cover: © dikkenss/Shutterstock; page 5: © Cheryl Quigley/Dreamstime.com; page 7: © Sara Julin Ingelmark/Shutterstock; page 9: © Alexey Stiop/Shutterstock; page 11: © gabriel12/Shutterstock; page 12: © Kelsey Fox/Shutterstock; page 17: © Sketchart/Shutterstock; page 18: © Kent Weakley/Shutterstock; page 19: © gabriel12/Shutterstock; page 23: © Stefan Holm/Shutterstock; page 24: © Dziurek/Shutterstock; page 27: © Amy Harris/Dreamstime.com; page 28 (top): © Elya Vatel/Shutterstock; page 28 (bottom): © Vladimir Hodac/Shutterstock

45th Parallel Press is an imprint of Cherry Lake Publishing Group.

Library of Congress Cataloging-in-Publication Data

Names: Gitlin, Marty, author.
Title: Ticket to the Triple Crown / Martin Gitlin.
Description: Ann Arbor, Michigan : Cherry Lake Publishing, [2023] | Series:
   The big game | Includes index. | Audience: Grades 4-6 | Summary: "Who
   has won the Triple Crown for horse racing? What horses made history?
   Written as high interest with struggling readers in mind, this series
   includes considerate vocabulary, engaging content and fascinating facts,
   clear text and formatting, and compelling photos. Educational sidebars
   include extra fun facts and information about each race. Includes table
   of contents, glossary, index, and author biography"-- Provided by
   publisher.
Identifiers: LCCN 2022039953 | ISBN 9781668919552 (hardcover) | ISBN
   9781668920572 (paperback) | ISBN 9781668921906 (ebook) | ISBN
   9781668923238 (pdf)
Subjects: LCSH: Triple Crown (U.S. horse racing)--History--Juvenile
   literature. | Race horses--United States--History--Juvenile literature.
   | Horse racing--United States--History--Juvenile literature.
Classification: LCC SF357.T74 G58 2023 | DDC 798.4--dc23/eng/20220928
LC record available at https://lccn.loc.gov/2022039953

Cherry Lake Publishing would like to acknowledge the work of the Partnership for 21st Century Learning, a network of Battelle for Kids. Please visit http://www.battelleforkids.org/networks/p21

Printed in the United States of America
Corporate Graphics

Table of Contents

Introduction

Horse racing is not as popular as some sports in the United States. Some people visit a track once in a while. It is where horse races are run. People visit to bet on which horse will win.

But interest goes way up 3 times a year. That is when Triple Crown events are held. Millions watch on TV. About 400,000 fans attend the events in person.

The Triple Crown begins with the Kentucky Derby. It is the most famous. It is held the first Saturday in May. It takes place at Churchill Downs in Louisville, Kentucky.

The second is the Preakness Stakes. That takes place 2 weeks after the Derby. It is held at Pimlico Race Course in Baltimore, Maryland.

The 2009 Kentucky Derby winner was jockey Calvin Borel. He won on a horse named Mine That Bird.

The last is the Belmont Stakes. It is run 2 weeks after the Preakness. The track is Belmont Park in Elmont, New York.

Only 3-year-old horses run Triple Crown races. They are the fastest in the United States. The greatest horses in history have won those events.

All 3 races are about the same distance. The horses run slightly more than 1 mile (1.6 kilometers). The Preakness is the shortest race. The Belmont is the longest.

Every horse has a rider known as a jockey. Jockeys guide the horses during the race. They are always light. Horses run faster without much weight on them.

Many people bet on Triple Crown races. They put money on horses to win. Or they bet on horses to finish second or third.

If they are right, they make money. If they are wrong, they lose money. But they all enjoy watching the horses run.

Jockeys speed on their horses toward the finish line.

A Bit of History

All 3 Triple Crown races began in the 1860s and 1870s. But they were not then known as the Triple Crown.

The term was first used in 1930. Charles Hatton was a reporter for the *New York Times*. Hatton used the term to combine all 3 races. In 1930, Gallant Fox won each race.

That was 63 years after the first Belmont Stakes. It was first run in 1867. It is the third-oldest horse race in America.

The Preakness came next. It was first held in 1873. That was 3 years after the Pimlico track opened.

The last was the Kentucky Derby. It was first run on May 17, 1875. That was the day Churchill Downs opened.

All 3 races got more popular. More people became interested in them as time went on. Hatton thought they were the most important races. That is why he called them the Triple Crown.

orey Lanerie rides a horse named Rajpur oad around the track at Churchill owns. Churchill Downs is where the entucky Derby takes place.

Often the same horses race all 3. But they must be 3 years old. They can never run them more than once.

Aristides won the first Kentucky Derby in 1875. He ran it in 2 minutes and 37 seconds. Racehorses soon became much faster. Old Rosebud won in 1914. His time was 2:03.

Secretariat was the first horse to break 2 minutes. In 1973, he finished at 1:59. Many believe he is the greatest racehorse ever. No horse has run it faster through 2022.

Secretariat did not only dominate the Derby. He ran the Preakness at 1:53. That remains its fastest time 49 years later. Pimlico is a bit shorter track than Churchill Downs.

Belmont is the longest race of the three. It became 1.5 miles (2.4 km) in 1926. It is no surprise that Secretariat holds the record. His time was 2:24.

Secretariat won Belmont easily. He put amazing distance between himself and the other horses. TV cameras showed him so far ahead that it shocked viewers.

Secretariat still holds the record for fastest Kentucky Derby finish at 1 minute, 59 seconds.

Triple Crown winners are rare. There are only 13 winners through 2022.

It has been done only twice since 1978. American Pharoah won all 3 in 2015. Justify did the same in 2018.

Sir Barton was the first to do it. He won all 3 races in 1919. But he was not known as a Triple Crown champion. He won the races before the Triple Crown was named.

The 1930s had 3 Triple Crown winners. One was Gallant Fox. The next was Omaha in 1935. War Admiral won it in 1937.

Triple Crown winner American Pharoah poses for the camera.

The Belmont Stakes race began in 1867.

Only 2 U.S. races are older than the Belmont.

The Phoenix Stakes began in 1831.

The Travers Stakes at Saratoga Race Course was first run in 1864. That was in Saratoga Springs, New York.

WAY BACK WHEN

Four horses won every race in the 1940s. That decade had the most Triple Crown winners. The first was Whirlaway in 1941. Count Fleet did it in 1943. Assault won the Triple Crown in 1946. Citation took it in 1948.

Many experts believe only 2 horses rival Secretariat. Some feel Citation is the greatest racehorse ever. Others give the nod to Man o' War. That horse won the 1920 Preakness and Belmont. He might have won the Derby as well. But he skipped that race.

Winning horses get most of the glory. But jockeys get credit as well. Only 1 has won 2 Triple Crowns. His name is Eddie Arcaro. He rode Whirlaway and Citation to all 3 victories. Many people believe he is the greatest jockey ever.

Arcaro and Bill Hartack each won 5 Kentucky Derby races. Arcaro has the most Preakness wins. He rode 6 horses to victories in that race. His 6-win streak is also tied for the most at Belmont. Jim McLaughlin also won 6. He won those in the 1800s.

Female racehorses are called fillies. None has ever won a Triple Crown. But many have won races.

 The first was Ruthless. She won the first Belmont in 1867. Only 2 fillies have won that race since. Just 23 raced in the Belmont through 2022.

 Three fillies have won the Kentucky Derby.

But the best race for fillies has been the Preakness. Five have taken that event.

A BIT OF !TRIVIA

The Best Battles

It was 1998. A horse named Real Quiet was expected to win the Triple Crown. He had taken the Kentucky Derby and Preakness. He was ahead of the pack in the Belmont.

The race was almost over. Real Quiet sped to the finish. Then it happened. Victory Gallop began to gallop fast. He closed the gap. He pulled up next to Real Quiet.

The 2 horses ran neck and neck. They ended the race that way. It was too close to call. It took a close-up photo to decide. And the photo showed that Victory Gallop had won.

Real Quiet lost the Triple Crown. But horse racing fans had a race to remember. Some believe it was the best ever.

Real Quiet and Victory Gallop raced neck and neck toward the finish line of Belmont Stakes. Victory Gallop won.

Horseshoes make horse hooves stronger and keep them protected. This is very important for racehorses!

Others feel the 1978 Belmont was better. That one featured 2 super horses. They were Affirmed and Alydar.

Affirmed had already won the first 2 Triple Crown races. But Alydar placed second in both. Most believed the Belmont would be close. And it sure was.

Sometimes races are close. Horses can be side by side until the finish line.

The 2 horses ran side by side. They pulled away from the pack. Alydar moved just ahead. Then Affirmed took the lead. And he remained just in front at the finish.

Affirmed had won the Triple Crown. But Alydar gained fame. He placed second in every Triple Crown race. No other horse did that.

The 1933 Kentucky Derby was not just a horse race. It was a fight to the finish. And the horses were not the only ones battling. So were the jockeys!

One was Don Meade. He was riding Brokers Tip. The other was Herb Fisher. He was on Head Play.

The 2 horses were heading to the wire. They were running first and second. The horses were side by side. Meade and Fisher began fighting each other. Brokers Tip won the race.

That did not end the fight. The 2 men continued to fight in the jockeys room.

AMAZING MOMENT

The Big Surprises

Underdogs are horses not expected to win. Some underdogs are picked to finish way behind. Or even to finish last.

But some underdogs surprise everyone. And they do win. When they win it is called an upset.

One underdog that pulled an upset was Donerail. He won the 1913 Kentucky Derby.

Owner Thomas Hayes did not even want him to enter. Jockey Roscoe Goose begged Hayes to let him run. A friend of Hayes put up the entry fee. So Hayes allowed Donerail to race.

Sometimes horses that aren't expected to win DO win! These horses are called underdogs.

Jockeys line up on their horses at the starting gate. The gate stalls open at the same time when the race begins.

He was glad he did. Donerail had about a 100–1 chance of winning. He was behind much of the race. Three other horses were ahead near the end. Then Donerail sped past all of them.

The crowd went crazy. A lucky few bet $2 on Donerail to win. They won nearly $200. That would be about $6,000 in today's dollars.

★ Legendary Man o' War had a rival. It was 1919 Triple Crown winner Sir Barton. They raced each other on October 12, 1920. No other horses were in the field.

★ The battle gained great attention. It was called "The Race of the Century." It was held in Canada. Nearly everyone believed Man o' War would win.

★ Sir Barton moved ahead early. But Man o' War bolted in front. He stayed in the lead and won easily.

★ His owner won $75,000. It was the largest prize ever given for an American horse at that time.

LEGENDS OF THE SPORT

The crowd also went crazy 109 years later. It was the same event. And a huge underdog pulled another upset.

His name was Rich Strike. He was supposed to finish close to last. Or maybe even last. But he shocked the horse racing world in 2022.

Epicenter and Zandon were the favorites. They were the horses expected to win.

Rich Strike almost did not run at all. Another horse was scratched. That means he was pulled out of the race. That allowed Rich Strike to run.

Epicenter was leading near the finish. That was no surprise. Then Rich Strike bolted from the pack. He raced past Epicenter and Zandon to win.

A few folks had bet $2 on Rich Strike. They took home $163. There was only 1 bigger upset in Derby history. And that was Donerail winning in 1913.

Sometimes horses can move up in the pack to pull ahead into the lead. This is what happened with Rich Strike at the Kentucky Derby.

The bit in the horse's mouth helps the jockey steer the horse.

Jockeys are hard workers. They train for more than 4 hours every day. They love what they do!

Huge upsets have shocked crowds in other Triple Crown races. One was the 1999 Preakness. Charismatic pulled off the upset.

It should not have been a huge surprise. Charismatic had already won the Derby. He had fallen way behind. But he surged to catch up.

Then came the Preakness. Charismatic was a huge underdog. More than 100,000 fans watched at Pimlico. He fell way behind. Then he bolted ahead near the finish. He passed horses one by one. And he won.

Charismatic had a shot at the Triple Crown. He needed to win the Belmont. He was finally given respect. Charismatic was favored to win. But he placed third.

Activity

Go online and read about any Triple Crown winner. Find out how he was trained. Learn about how he lived out his life after racing. Then ask your teacher if you can write about that horse.

Learn More

BOOKS

Green, John. *Great Racehorses Coloring Book: Triple Crown Winners and Other Champions*. Mineola, NY: Dover Publications, 2016.

Hubbard, Crystal. *The Last Black King of the Kentucky Derby*. New York: Lee & Low Books, 2008.

Wilbur, Helen L. *D is for Derby: A Kentucky Derby Alphabet*. Ann Arbor, MI: Sleeping Bear Press, 2014.

WEBSITES

Britannica Kids: Horse Racing: https://kids.britannica.com/students/article/horse-racing/274949

Indy with Kids: A Day at the Horse Races Is Family Fun: https://indywithkids.com/horseraces/

Kiddle: Kentucky Derby Facts for Kids: https://kids.kiddle.co/Kentucky_Derby

Glossary

favorites (FAY-vuh-ruhts) horses expected to win races

fillies (FIH-leez) female racehorses

jockey (JAH-kee) rider who guides a racehorse

scratched (SKRACHD) removed from the field of a horse race

track (TRAK) oval on which horses run races

underdogs (UHN-duhr-dawgs) horses given little chance to win

upset (UHP-set) unexpected win by a horse

Index

About the Author

Marty Gitlin is a sports book author based in Cleveland. He won more than 45 awards as a newspaper sportswriter from 1991 to 2002. Included was a first-place award from the Associated Press for his coverage of the 1995 World Series. He has had more than 200 books published since 2006. Most of them were written for students.